dedication

To my dear wife and
family whose presence
has been my joy and
to my students who
allow me to share my
knowledge.

the history

Arnis the Filipino art of stick fighting, which
also includes the use of bladed weapons was
introduced to the Philippines around 200 B.C.
by the Malays who migrated to the southern
islands of the Philippines in Sulu and Mindanao.
The art of the Malay consisted mainly of bladed
weapons known as Kali. Although the Malayians
were skilled in bladed weapons they were also
skilled in sticks and empty hand arts. This no
doubt was greatly influenced by their contact
with Chinese merchants whom they had estab-
lished business relationships. When the Spanish
colonized the Philippines, kali was forced under-
grounds and practiced in secret. It was furthered
developed and when it emerged in the open it was
disguised in the form of moro-moro plays and
other dramatic presentations in mock combat with
the blades. Many systems were developed from
the original art of kalis. Later it was known as
kali. As the various arts from kali were developed it was later called Arnis. The word Arnis
is derived from the Spanish word arnes, meaning
"harness". Although the word is misleading, it
was an effort by the Spanish to describe the actor's
hand motions as he gracefully moved the trappings
during a performance for the Spaniards. Today
Arnis is practiced widely in the Philippines and
like its sister arts of karate and kung fu there are
many systems, depending on the region and pro-
vince. However, there are three basic forms that
are popular. There is the sword and dagger style
or espada y daga. Instead of the wooden sword
and dagger, the modern practitioner uses the
long and short sticks. The second style is the use
of the long stick. The left hand is free to trap and

ARNIS

FILIPINO ART OF STICK

FIGHTING

by

ABU JALMAANI
JUN GARCIA

First Printing 1976
Second Printing 1977
Third Printing 1978
Fourth Printing 1979

———————■———————

KOINONIA PRODUCTIONS
Stockton, California

table of contents

block. This single stick art is popular with the Pangasinense, Ilocanos, Viajeros, and natives of Batangas. And then a third form of Arnis is called the sinawali, it is the use of two sticks. This is the most difficult style to master because of the intricate movements and extreme coordination required.

Today there are many open contest in Arnis in the Philippines. The contestants wear gloves and chest pads. A point is scored when one of the contestants can score a controlled point to any vital areas. Rules varied from region to region. Like karate in its infancy stage in the United States, standardization of rules in sports Arnis will be the enevitable results if the sport continues to grow. A regular television program features karate and arnis contests are viewed by the public each Sunday afternoon on one of Philippines major television stations. The program sponsored by the Philippine Karate and Arnis Association is gaining in popularity. Arnis is taught in the physical education program of every school in Manila.

Although Arnis is still an unknown art in the United States, it will find its place in the main - stream of the martial arts world in the United States because several expert teachers have migrated to the United States. This book is the first in a series to deal with the art of stick and blade fighting.

the author

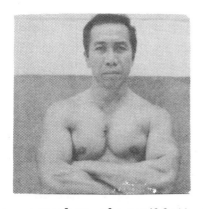

Abubakar Jalmaani was born in Jolo Mindanao on the southern tip of the Philippine Islands. His involvement in the various martial arts and athletic activities at an early age was natural. As member of an athletic family Abu found his daily recreation in the waters of the Pacific and the long hours of training in Arnis and Silat. When he reached adulthood, he discovered that the early training as a boy was responsible for his athletic efficiency and his coordination and flexibility helped him to win the tryouts to represent the Philippines in the 1964 Olympics in Japan in swimming. In 1972 and 1973 Abu won the Mr. Philippines title in bodybuilding and also competed two successive years, placing high in the Mr. Asia contest against eighteen nations. Since his retirement from active competition he continues to train three hours a day in the Martial arts and also teach at Adamson University. In addition to his busy schedule he has squeezed in starring roles in several movies, two of which is being shown in the United States, and teaches Arnis and Silat.

The author practicing movements from a Silat form

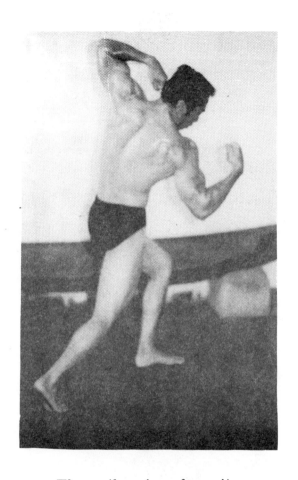

The author in a favorite
pose that won him the
title of "Mr. Philippines"
in 1972-73

author

JUN GARCIA

Jun Garcia is a native of Manila. He has studied many forms of martial arts since the age of twelve. He is an actor by profession and has appeared in over twenty movies, among them are, "The Bamboo Trap", "The Undefeated", "The Pacific Connection" (an Arnis movie with such stars as, Alejandro Rey, Guy Madison, Gilbert Roland, and Dean Stockwell), and "Apocalyse Now" starring Marlon Brando. In addition to studying many styles of Arnis, he holds a fifth degree black belt in Okinawa karate. He is an expert in the nunchaku and tonfa. Mr. Garcia and Mr. Jalmaani are heads of the Philippines Stuntmen's Organization, a group trained to provide stuntmen for films.

8

introduction

After over thirty years of invovlement in the martial arts in general and silat and arnis in particular. I have seen the various fighting arts emerged from behind the scene of anonymity to take its place in the main stream of the world's activities. We now see karate, kung fu, judo and arnis in the movies to give the scenes more sensationalism. Religious orders see the value in martial arts as an effective tool for developing the spirit. Social scientists acknowledged martial arts as an effective instrument for developing self discipline in rebellious youth. As the martial arts becomes more open, the intermingling of techniques and philosophies become more prevalent. This inter-change of ideas have been responsible for the refinement of the various arts. It is my philosophy and personal conviction that each art has something to contribute to the total. It is with this in mind that I present this first volume on Arnis. This volume is not intended to be an elaborate or detailed text. It is merely an introduction to thirty six years of practice in the fighting art. To share thirty six years of practice and discovery would take more than one volume to say the least. However, after thirty six years, I have discovered that the key to effective application of ones knowledge in this art lies in SIMPLICITY.

A. Jalmaani

STRIKES

STRIKING OF ARNIS

Striking in Arnis is the heart of the system. This is not to say that offense takes precedence over defense. But it is saying that once one learns the various angles of attack, that person will be more familiar with all the variables in a combat situation. Defense and counter begins with a knowledge of offense. Once the practitioner is acquainted with attacking, he becomes aware of his opponent's capabilities and how he deals with it from there on will determine the ulmate outcome.

The number of basic strikes in the art of Arnis is determined by the system one practice. Some have as few as six and others as many as twelve. I have added an extra angle and therefore advocate thirteen strikes for the sake of practice. However, it is our belief that as one becomes more proficient, numbers are immaterial. Scoring on an opponent is determined more by timing, speed, reflex action than by variety. In order to reach that stage of proficiency one must begin with the excess and evolve to the stage of simplicity.

TEMPLE STRIKE

1a

1b

(1a) With feet approximately twelve to fifteen inches apart, keep left hand chest high for trapping and the stick in a ready position. Eyes should be focused on the chest •

(1b) Execute a strike to the temple by turning the body to the left and snapping the wrist. Right foot can be to the rear or as the lead foot, depends on personal preference.

REVERSE TEMPLE STRIKE

(2a) From ready position, bring the stick over to the left shoulder and left hand held chest high.
(2b) Strike to the opponent's right temple.

ARM STRIKE

3a

3b

(3a) From ready position, bring
stick back to horizonal position
behind the head and left hand held
chest high.
(3b) Swing toward left and strike
opponent on the elbow. Please
note, always strike to bony areas
of the body.

REVERSE ARM STRIKE

(4a) From ready position bring the
stick over to the left shoulder and
keep left hand chest high.
(4b) Strike the opponent's right
elbow by swinging to the right with
a twistng motion of the wrist as
the stick lands.

KNEE STRIKE

(5a) From ready position bring the stick back to the back of the head , with left hand held chest high.
(5b) Swing the stick down to the bony areas of the knee.

REVERSE KNEE STRIKE

(6a) From ready position bring the striking hand over to the left shoulder and left hand held chest high.

(6b) Swing the stick downward to the bony areas of the knee.

GROIN SWEEP STRIKE

(7a) From ready position bring the
stick to a horizontal position to
the head. With eyes focused on the
opponent and left hand held chest
high, without giving away your in-
tention set for groin strike.
(7b) From ready position sweep the
stick down and up to the opponent's
groin area. Deception is key in this
strike.

REVERSE GROIN SWEEP STRIKE

(8a) From ready position bring the stick back to the left shoulder. The strike is similiar to number 7b. (8b) Strike by executing a reverse sweep down and up to the opponent's groin.

(9a) From ready position bring the stick back to a horizontal and at the same times keep eyes focused on opponent's chest area.
(9b) Execute a straight jab to the opponent's left eye.

(10a) From ready position bring stick across to the front of the chin, palm up, focus on the opponent and left hand held high. (10b) Strike a straight jab to the opponent's right eye.

COLLAR STRIKE

(11a) From ready position rest the stick on the back of the neck. With left hand held chest high focus eyes on opponent.
(11b) Strike down to the collar bone by slightly turning the wrist as you strike.

REVERSE COLLAR STRIKE

(12a) From ready position bring the stick to the left shoulder. (12b) Strike down to the right collar bone with the snap of the wrist.

OVERHEAD STRIKE

(13a) From a ready position hold the stick slightly over the head.
(13b) Strike down to the crown of the head.

BLOCKING

CROSS BLOCK

(14) From a ready stance, attacker in white uniform readies for a upward sweep to the groin.
(14a) Defender in black blocks by crossing the two sticks and trapping the attacking stick.

OUTSIDE BLOCK

(15) From a ready stance, attacker set to attack with a strike to the temple.

(15a) Defender blocks the strike by executing an outward block with the left stick.

(16) Attacker assumes ready position
to attack defender with overhead strike.
(16a) As attacker strikes with overhead
strike, defender blocks with left hand,
and turns body slightly to the right.

(17) Attacker assumes ready position to attack defender with sweeping knee strike.

(17a) Defender blocks attacker by bringing the left stick down to meet the attack and turn slightly to the left as the sticks make contact.

UPPER CROSS BLOCK

(18) Attacker assumes ready position to attack defender with overhead strike. (18a) As attacker strikes, defender blocks with a cross block by bringing the right stick over the left and catching the attackers stick in the center.

DOWNWARD BLOCK

(19) Attacker attempts an inside chest strike. Defender blocks with left block.

(20) Attacker attempts lower groin sweep. Defender blocks with lower block.

(21) Attacker attempts a strike to
the right collar. Defender blocks
with horizontal block.

(22) Attacker attempts lower knee
sweeping attack. Defender blocks
with lower block by turning the
body slightly to the left upon contact
of the sticks.

HORIZONTAL BLOCK

(23) Attacker attempts left attack to collar bone. Defender blocks by moving slightly to the left upon contact of the sticks.

(24) Attacker attempts straight jab to eye. Defender parry by bringing the stick up to a verticle position.

CROSS BLOCK

(25) Attacker attempts left sweep groin attack. Defender blocks with a Cross block.

BLOCK & HIT

(26) Attacker attempts an arm
strike. Defender blocks.
(26a) Defender counters with a
left strike to attacker's elbow
area.

HORIZONTAL BLOCK ELBOW STRIKE

(27) Attacker attempts strike to temple. Defender blocks with horizontal block.
(27a) Defender counters with a sweeping upward strike to the attacker's elbow.

CROSS BLOCK ARM STRIKE

(28) Attacker attempts an elbow strike. Defender blocks with a verticle block.
(28a) As defender blocks immediately counter with a arm strike.

FRONT BLOCK WRIST STRIKE

(29) Attacker attempts an outward strike to the temple. Defender blocks.
(29a) Defender counters with a strike to attacker's wrist.

CROSS BLOCK KNUCKLE STRIKE

30

30a

(30) Attacker attempts a groin
sweep to the defender's groin.
Defender blocks with cross
block.
(30a) Defender counters with a
strike to attacker's knuckles.

31

31a

(31) Attacker attempts a strike to defender's knee. Defender blocks.
(31a) Defender counters with a strike to attacker's wrist.

OUTSIDE BLOCK WRIST STRIKE

(32) Attacker attempts a jab to defender's eye. Defender blocks with a verticle block.
(32a) Defender counters with a strike to attacker's arm.

(33) Attacker attempts a jab to defender's eye. Defender blocks with verticle block. (33a) Defender counters with a strike to attacker's arm.

DOWNWARD BLOCK WRIST STRIKE

(34) Attacker attempts a groin sweep to defender's groin area. Defender block by stepping back with left foot. (34a) Defender counter by striking to attacker's wrist.

OUTSIDE BLOCK ELBOW STRIKE

(35) Attacker attempts a eye jab to defender's eye. Defender blocks.
(35a) Defender counters with an upper elbow sweep strike to attacker's elbow.

DISARMING

36

36a

(36) Attacker on the right (in black)
attempts an overhead strike. Defender
blocks with an inside block.
(36a) Defender disarms attacker by
grabbing the stick in the left hand and
with the right stick slide down and
strike opponent on the hand and jerk
with the left at the sametime.

(36b) As defender freed opponent's stick, pull back into a ready position.
(36c) And counter with an overhead strike to the crown of the head.

(37) As attacker attempts an overhead strike, defender blocks.
(37a) Defender grabs attacker's stick and pulls, using the right stick as a fulcrum, prepare to disarm.

(37b) Pull with left hand and jerk up with the right hand, holding the stick in a semi-verticale position.

(37c) Defender counters with an overhead strike.

(38) Attacker attempts an upward groin sweep. Defender blocks with a downward block.
(38a) Defender grabs opponent's stick with left hand and pull.

38b

38c

(38b) Defender lift up with the right hand and pull down and in with the left hand.
(38c) Defender counters with a right temple strike.

(38d) Defender follow through with strike to temple.

(39) Attacker strikes with an over-head strike. Defender blocks with right hand and grabs attacker's stick with the left.

(39a) Defender turns the right hand
and with the butt of the stick brings
the stick down on the attacker's
wrist and jerks the stick from the
attacker's hand at the sametime.
(39b) As defender jerks away, he
assumes a ready position for a
counter strike。

(39c) Defender counters with a overhead strike。

(40) Attacker strikes with a swing to the defender's temple. Defender blocks.

55

(40a) Defender grabs simultanouesly as he blocks.
(40b) Using the right stick as a ful-crum, defender jerks stick from attacker's hand.

(40c) Defender counters with strike to attacker's temple.

(41) Attacker attempts an overhead strike. Defender blocks with a horizontal block.

(41a) Maintaining contact with the
stick after the block, defender scoops
over and under attacker's stick.
(41b) Continuing the motion in 41a,
defender traps attacker's stick under
his arm.

(41c) Defender in a verticle motion jerks the stick from the attacker's hand by turning the body slightly to the right.

(42) Attacker attempts an overhead strike. Defender blocks.

(42a) From 42 slide the right
stick down and jerk up, using
the right stick as a fulcrum.
(42b) Defender in a position to
counter.

(42c) From 42b defender counters with a temple strike.

(43) Attacker attempts an overhead strike. Defender blocks.

(43a) From 43 defender grabs attacker's stick and at the same time slide the right stick down.

(43b) From 43a pull down with the left hand and push up with the right stick to break attacker's grip.

DISARM - KNEE STRIKE

(44) Attacker attempts a knee strike and a shoulder strike, (44a) defender blocks both.

(44b) Defender grabs attacker's stick and slides right stick down. (44c) In a slightly outward motion with the right hand, defender jerks with the left to disarm.

(44d) From 44c defender counters
with a temple strike.

45

45a

(45) Attacker in white attempts a right temple strike. Defender in a defensive posture.

(45a) As attacker strikes, defender moves to his left and parries the attacking hand, immobilizing the attacker's stick with the right hand.

(45b) From 45a defender brings his
left foot back and simultaneously
bends the attacker's stick toward
him and pulling forward.
(45c) From 45b defender jerks back.
From this position defender can
counter.

(46) As attacker attempts an overhead strike, shift to the outside of attacker's line of attack and trap his arm with both hands.
(46a) Maintain a grip with the left hand and ready the right hand for circling around the stick.

(46b) From 46a circle the stick
and maintain a grip with the arms
and pull out with the body to disarm.

(47) As attacker strikes with an
overhead strike, step inside and
block with right arm.

(47a) From 47 maintain a grip
with the left arm and execute a
hammer fist strike to the ribs.
(47b) From 47a continue the
attack with a backfist to the jaw.

70

(47c) From 47b trap the stick by
sliding the right fist down and
grabbing the stick with the left
hand.

(48) Attacker attempts to execute
a straight jab. Defender in a defensive position.

(48a) As attacker lunges, defender step slightly to the left and grabs stick with both hands.
(48b) From 48a defender quickly turn the stick to the left towards the attacker.

(48c) From 48b defender jerks the stick away from attacker and in a posture to counter.

(49) Attacker attempts an overhead strike. Defender in a defensive position.

(49a) As attacker strikes, step in
and block with a right inside block
and trap the stick with the left hand.
(49b) From 49a push the stick up
with the left hand and slide the right
down to disarm.

(50) Attacker attempts strike to the temple, defender in defensive posture.
(50a) As attacker strikes defender steps inside and block, trapping the opponent's arm with the left hand.

(50b) From 50a defender counters with an elbow strike to the ribs.

(51) Attacker executes an overhead strike. Defender steps in and parries.

(51a) From 51 defender grabs stick and turn in a counterclock wise direction and disarm。

(52) Attacker executes an overhead strike。 Defender blocks and traps with the left open hand。

52a

52b

(52a) From 52 defender steps in
and bring right hand under opponent's
elbow.
(52b) From 52a defender pull down
with the left and pull up with the
right.

(52c) From 52b defender jerks
away to disarm.

DEFENSE AGAINST EYE THRUST

(53) Attacker attempts to execute
a straight thrust to the eye. Defender
in a defensive posture.

(53a) From 53 as attacker lunges
step slightly to the left and parry
and immobilizing the attacking arm.
(53b) From 53a turn the stick toward
the attacker.

(53c) From 53b jerk back to disarm.
Defender is in position to counter.

DEFENSE AGAINST TEMPLE STRIKE

(54) Attacker executes a swing to
the temple. Defender blocks with
inside block.

(54a) From 54 quickly snap the right
arm inward and push forward with
the left to disarm。

KNIFE

DEFENSE

(55) Attacker in white attempts to
execute an overhead knife attack.
Defender in a defensive position.
(55a) From 55 as attacker lunge
forward, defender steps to the
left and simultaneously strike the
attacker on the wrist. Notice: all
arnis strikes are with a snapping
wrist action. Do not over commit
the body.

(56) Attacker attempts a lunge attack.
(56a) As attacker lunges, defender
shift to the right in a semi-counter-
clockwise direction and simultaneously
strike to the wrist.

(57) Opponent attempts an outward slash with the knife. Defender assumes a defensive posture.

(57a) As opponent attack, defender steps to the side and strikes opponent on the wrist.

(58) Attacker attempts an overhead strike. Defender assumes defensive posture.
(58a) As attacker strikes, defender shift to the right and strikes attacker on the wrist.

(59) Attacker attempts an inward slash. Defender in a defensive position.

(59a) As opponent slash, defender pivot to the right and strike simultaneously to the wrist.

(60) Opponent attempts to execute a straight stab. Defender assumes a defensive position.
(60a) As opponent lunge, defender pivot to the right and strike to attacker's wrist.

(61)Opponent attempts a straight stab. Defender assumes defensive position.
(61a) As opponent lunge, defender step to the right and execute an inward strike to the attacker's wrist.

(62) Attacker attempts a straight stab. Defender assumes a defensive position.
(62a) As attacker lunges, defender executes an overhand strike, as he pulls the left foot back.

(63) Attacker attempts an overhead stab. Defender assumes defensive position.

(63a) As attacker lunges, defender steps to the left and executes an upper strike to the elbow.

WEIGHT
TRAINING

There are many myths and wives
tales about the negative results of
using weights for training. What-
ever disadvantages in using weights,
it is outweighed by the positives.
Training with weights can give an
athlete a decided advantage that can-
not be gained by just limiting one to
practicing the art alone. The power,
muscle tone and physique resulting
from a systematic program of exercises is worth the risk. The world
wide acceptance of weight training
in various sports is indicative of the
tremendous positive results of such
a program. Weight training can be
the key to reaching a higher plateau
in Arnis.

The exercises on the following pages
are merely basics that a beginner can
follow. Begin by doing ten repetitions
of three sets of each exercise. Start
with a weight that is comfortable increase poundage as the weights gets
lighter. If you are seeking a well defined
body, increase the repetitions instead
of the poundage. If you are seeking a
bulky body, increase the poundage and
lower the repetitions.

BENCH PRESS

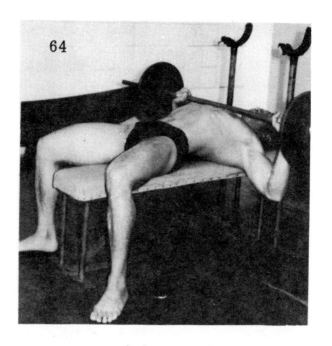

(64) Bring the barbell down to the chest. Take a deep breath and push up and exhale as illustrated in the next page in figure 64a.

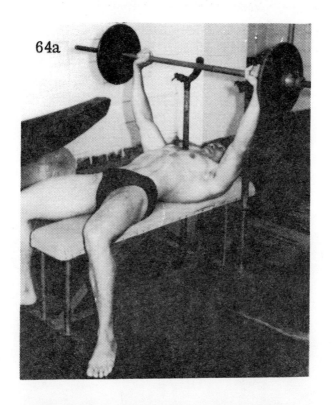

(64a) From 64 exhale and slowly
let down to the chest. Repeat for
ten repetition. Start with a weight
that is comfortable and add weight
as each repetition becomes easier.

PUSH UPS BETWEEN CHAIRS

(65) Using two chairs and supporting
the feet on a bench or another chair
and spacing each chair thirty inches
apart assume a push up position.

(65a) Keeping back straight push up
and exhale. Repeat for ten repetition.
Increase reps as exercise gets easier.
Be sure to inhale on the way down
and exhale at the completion of the
rep.

PULL OVERS

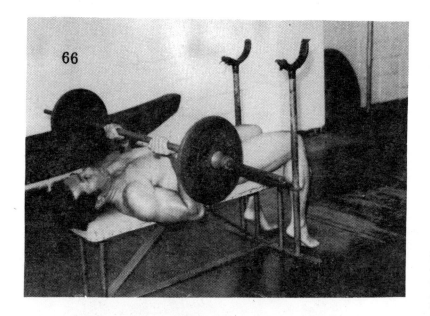

66

(66) From a prone position bring the barbell to the chest, brace legs on the edge of the bench.

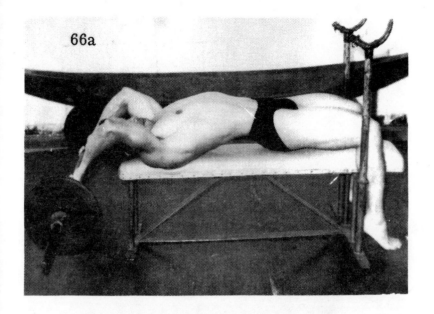

66a

(66a) From 66 inhale and let the bar down behind the head and touch the floor and then pull back to the original position and exhale. Repeat for about ten repetitions. Increase weight as exercise gets easier.

BENT OVER ROWINGS

(67) From a bend position. Keep the back straight and knees slightly bent. Look straight ahead.

(67a) From 67 inhale and pull barbell
to the chest and then lower and exhale.
Repeat for ten repetition.

CHIN BEHIND THE NECK

(68) Grip the chinning bar, with palm
facing out, as wide as you can.

(68a) From 68 inhale and pull up touch-
ing the back of the neck. Exhale as
you lower and repeat for ten repetition.
Increase reps as exercise gets easier.

BARBELL ARM CURLS

(69) Grip bar with palms facing up and feet about eighteen inches apart.

(69a) From 69 inhale and curl bar to
the chest. Keep back straight. Lower
and exhale. Repeat for ten repetitions.

TRICEP CURLS

(70) Hold bar with hands about six inches apart, with palms facing up and lower the barbell behind the neck.

(70a) Exhale as you curl the bar up over the head and inhale as you lower the bar. repeat for about ten repetition.

(71) Clean the barbell to the chest, holding it with palms up. Inhale as you squat.

71a

(71a) From 71 squat and return to a standing position and exhale. Repeat for ten repetition.

INCLINE SIT UPS

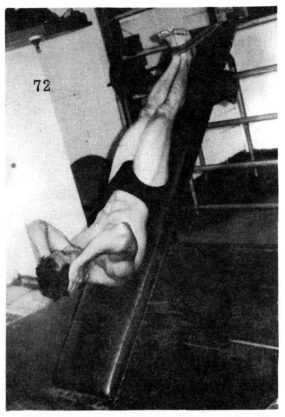

(72) From an incline position on the situp board, inhale and sit up. Repeat for about ten to twenty reps.